A Robbie Reader

Meet Our New Student From NEW ZEALAND

Ann Weil

Mitchell Lane
PUBLISHERS

P.O. Box 196
Hockessin, Delaware 19707
Visit us on the web: www.mitchelllane.com
Comments? email us: mitchelllane@mitchelllane.com

Mitchell Lane PUBLISHERS

Meet Our New Student From

Australia • China • Colombia • Great Britain
• Haiti • Israel • Korea • Malaysia • Mexico
• **New Zealand** • Nigeria • Tanzania

For all my friends in New Zealand, especially Dorothy Strong and the Barrier-Piggott family. Thank you! –AW

PUBLISHER'S NOTE: The facts on which the story in this book is based have been thoroughly researched. Documentation of such research can be found on page 44. While every possible effort has been made to ensure accuracy, the publisher will not assume liability for damages caused by inaccuracies in the data, and makes no warranty on the accuracy of the information contained herein.

Printing   1   2   3   4   5   6   7   8   9

NOTE ON PRONUNCIATIONS: There is tremendous variation in how Maori words are pronounced in New Zealand. Also, the Maori vowel sounds are different from the way we pronounce vowels in America. For example, the *kah* or *hah* sound is almost like an expulsion of breath. In addition, Maori do not emphasize one syllable over another, as we do in English. I spoke with New Zealand friends over the phone to confirm the pronunciations in this book. –AW

Library of Congress Cataloging-in-Publication Data
Weil, Ann.
  Meet our new student from New Zealand / by Ann Weil.
    p. cm. — (A Robbie reader)
Includes bibliographical references and index.
ISBN 978-1-58415-657-4 (library bound)
1. New Zealand—Juvenile literature. I. Title.
DU408.W45 2008
993—dc22
                                        2008002809

PLB

CONTENTS

New Zealand

Stirling Falls in Milford
Sound, on New Zealand's
South Island. Glaciers
moving through South
Island left U-shaped
valleys and steep drops
like this one.

A Kiwi in Class

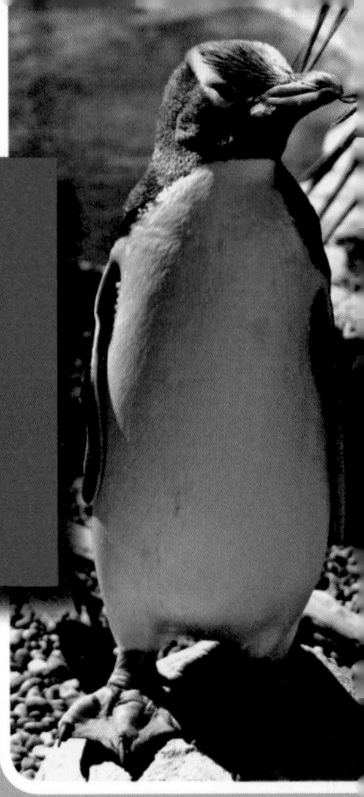

Why did Mr. Lorenz write *bungee jumping* on the board? Fred asked himself as he took his seat. Fred liked his third-grade teacher. Mr. Lorenz made learning even the boring stuff fun.

Mr. Lorenz continued writing:

Sheep
Kiwi
Maori
Rugby
Lord of the Rings

Fred heard some of his classmates giggling and whispering. Everyone was wondering what Mr. Lorenz was up to.

The teacher turned to face the class. "Okay, who can tell me what these things have in common?" he asked.

Bungee (BUN-jee) jumping, as a sport, was invented by AJ Hackett of New Zealand. Now it is popular all over the world. People jump off a bridge or other high place with a stretchy rope, called a bungee, attached to their body. The bungee stretches out, then snaps the jumper back up before he or she hits the ground. The jumper bounces up and down in the air, upside down, until the bungee stops.

Not a single hand went up.

Mr. Lorenz turned back to the board and wrote NEW ZEALAND across the top in big capital letters. "Does that help?" he asked.

"What's a New Zealand?" asked Nick.

"It's not a what," said Olivia. "It's a where."

"Exactly, Olivia," said Mr. Lorenz. "New Zealand is a country, a country we will study this week."

"I thought we were studying the water cycle this week," said Dylan.

"So you do listen to me after all, Dylan," Mr. Lorenz joked. "Yes, last week I did say we would study the water cycle this week. However, I changed my mind. I decided we would study New Zealand instead."

Kiwi fruit is grown in New Zealand, Italy, and the United States.

New Zealand is home to about 45 million sheep. That's more than ten times the number of people who live there.

Fred smiled. He knew Mr. Lorenz was waiting for someone in the class to ask why. "Why?" Fred said.

"I'm glad you asked that, young man," said Mr. Lorenz. "We will study New Zealand because we are lucky to have a new student from New Zealand. She and her family just moved here to Newark, Delaware, and she will join our class next week."

The class buzzed with excitement. Every hand shot up. Everyone had a question about New Zealand.

The Maori were the first people to live in New Zealand. Maori warriors would tattoo their faces and bodies.

The kiwi bird lives only in New Zealand. It grows to be about as big as a chicken. With its small wings, the kiwi cannot fly, but it can run very fast. It is active at night and not during the day. Look for two dots at the tip of its long, pointy bill. These are the bird's nostrils! The bird uses them to smell food as it pokes in the dirt.

The word *kiwi* (KEE-wee) has several meanings. It is a New Zealand bird. It is a fruit that grows in New Zealand. It is also the nickname for people from New Zealand.

"Where is it?" asked Ethan.

"What language do they speak?" asked Robin.

"Were there dinosaurs in New Zealand?" asked Kyle. Kyle was always wondering about dinosaurs.

"Those are good questions," said Mr. Lorenz. "And we will answer them all before the week is over."

The bell rang. It was time for recess. Fred loved recess, but he was sorry to leave the classroom. He wanted to know more about New Zealand, now.

20-cent New Zealand coin

As the class got ready to go outside, Mr. Lorenz finished. "Your homework for this week is to find out what these"—he pointed to the list he had written on the board—"have to do with New Zealand. Kyle, your extra credit assignment is to prepare a report on dinosaurs

Rugby is the national sport of New Zealand. It has ties to both football and soccer. The first rugby games were played in England in the 1800s.

New Zealand is home to six species of penguins. All penguins live south of the equator. Penguins have feathers and lay eggs. They use their "wings" (called flippers) to move through water, not air.

of New Zealand. And I expect you all to be able to find New Zealand on the map."

For the thousandth time, Fred was glad that Mr. Lorenz was his third-grade teacher. This was going to be a fun week.

New Zealand

EQUATOR
2066nm - 3827km

TROPIC OF CAPRICORN
659nm - 1220km

VANCOUVER
6229nm - 11434km

LOS ANGELES
5709nm - 10479km

BLUFF
756nm - 1401km

SYDNEY

New Zealand is a long way from everywhere else. Long ago, it took months at sea to reach these remote islands. Now people can fly from the United States to New Zealand in about 12 hours.

Aotearoa: Land of the Long White Cloud

Chapter 2

The first people to come to New Zealand were the **Maori** (maw-or-ee). They arrived by canoe about 750 years ago. They named their new home Aotearoa (ah-tee-ah-ROH-ha). That means "land of the long white cloud" in their language. Many people still use that name for New Zealand today.

The Maori tell stories of their first homeland, called Hawaiki (hah-wy-EE-kee, or ah-vah-EE-kee). They believed their gods lived there. In this magical place, people turned into animals. No one knows for sure where Hawaiki really was. The location of the **mythical** Hawaiki remains a mystery to this day.

Explorers from Europe

Explorers from Europe sailed to New Zealand in the 1600s. **Dutch** explorer Abel Tasman was the first European to discover New Zealand—but he did not set foot on land. Maori canoes came out to meet him

Detail of Islands

Norfolk Island
(AUSTRALIA)

KERMADEC
ISLANDS

THREE KINGS
ISLANDS

North
Island

Tasman
Sea

SOUTH
PACIFIC
OCEAN

NEW ZEALAND

CHATHAM
ISLANDS

South
Island

BOUNTY
ISLANDS

Stewart
Island

SNARES
ISLANDS

ANTIPODES ISLAND
GROUP

AUCKLAND
ISLANDS

Campbell
Island

300 Kilometers

300 Miles

Waitangi

Auckland

NORTH ISLAND

Tasman
Sea

Ruapehu
▲

Napier
•

Hawke

Wellington
★

PACIFIC OCEAN

Aoraki-Mount Cook
▲

Christchurch
•

SOUTH ISLAND

Where in the World

FACTS ABOUT NEW ZEALAND

Total Area: 103,737 square miles

(includes Antipodes Islands, Auckland Islands, Bounty Islands, Campbell Island, Chatham Islands, and Kermadec Islands)

Population: 4,250,000 (2007); about 80 percent of the people live in cities

Capital City: Wellington

Religions: Christian, Roman Catholic; over 25 percent practice no religion

Official Languages: English, Maori, New Zealand Sign Language

Industries: food processing, wood and paper products, textiles, machinery, transportation equipment, banking and insurance, tourism, mining

Chief Exports: dairy products, meat, wood and wood products, fish, machinery

Monetary Unit: New Zealand dollar (NZD)

and his men. At first, the Maori seemed friendly, but the two groups could not understand each other.

The Dutch sailed closer to land. Some of the Dutch sailors got into smaller boats to go ashore. More Maori canoes appeared. The Dutch sailors were nervous. Still, they could not talk to each other. Then one of the Maori canoes rammed into one of the smaller boats. Three Dutch sailors were killed. A fourth was badly hurt and later died from his wounds.

The Dutch fired their guns, but the Maori were already too far away. Quickly the Dutch prepared to leave. They raised anchor and set sail. Maori canoes chased them. The Dutch fired again. This time they hit a Maori warrior. The Maori canoes turned back to shore.

Other European explorers came later. British explorer James Cook arrived in New Zealand in 1769. French explorer Jean-François-Marie de Surville was there at the same time—but the British and French ships did not see each other.

Whales, Timber, and Flax

New Zealand had many valuable natural resources. It became an important whaling center in the early 1800s. The fat from whales, called blubber, was melted down to make oil. This oil was used in lamps, and some people used it to cook. Whale-oil lamps lit city streets at night.

Timber was another big **industry** in New Zealand around that time. The British Navy needed tall, straight tree trunks to build the masts of their ships. New Zealand forests were full of huge trees, perfect for this purpose. By the beginning of the 1800s, loggers were busy chopping them down.

Flax is a plant with many uses. The Maori used all parts of the plant. They wove the leaves to make mats and baskets. They drank the sweet nectar from its flowers. They crushed the roots to make medicines. Europeans used flax to make rope.

Maori bag woven from flax leaves

The Treaty of Waitangi

In 1840, more than 500 Maori chiefs in different parts of New Zealand signed a **treaty** with the **British Crown**. The treaty,

The Maori Meeting House on the Waitangi Historic Reserve, where the Treaty of Waitangi was signed in 1840. Although Waitangi Day is a national holiday, it is not marked by fun celebrations. Instead, it is a day to think about the treaty.

which offered the Maori rights and protection if they accepted British rule, was first signed in a place called Waitangi (wy-TANG-ee). It became known as the Treaty of Waitangi. This historic occasion is remembered every February 6. It is a national holiday called Waitangi Day. For many Maori, it is a day of mourning, and a time to reflect on broken promises.

New Zealand became independent from Britain in 1907.

New Zealand

Naturally hot water erupts in New Zealand. There used to be more than 200 of these erupting hot springs in New Zealand. Now there are fewer than 60.

New Zealand
Hot Spots

Chapter

There are active volcanoes in New Zealand. Earthquakes leave deep, long gashes in the ground. Geysers (GY-zurz) of boiling hot water spurt high into the air. The country also has snow-capped mountains with icy glaciers, calm ocean bays, and rain forests.

Earthquakes

New Zealand is on top of cracks in the earth's crust. The cracks separate huge chunks of land, called plates. When one plate bumps another, the earth rumbles and shakes.

New Zealand has many earthquakes. Most are not serious, but a few have been deadly. In 1931, a series of earthquakes struck the Hawke's Bay region of North Island. Buildings crumbled. Roofs caved in. People were crushed. More than 250 people died, and thousands were hurt. It was New Zealand's worst earthquake disaster.

Volcanoes

Active volcanoes and earthquakes often go together. New Zealand is on the Pacific Ring of Fire, which includes more than 75 percent of the world's volcanoes. Ruapehu (roo-ah-pay-hoo) is an active volcano on North Island. The name means a hole *(rua)* that explodes with a loud noise *(pehu)*. Ruapehu erupted in 1945. Then the **crater** filled with water. It is called Crater Lake.

On Christmas Eve, 1953, Ruapehu erupted again. One edge of Crater Lake crumbled. A huge amount of water roared into the river. It picked up rocks and mud as it flowed down the mountainside.

Mudflow from a volcano is called a **lahar** (LAH-har). A lahar can be even more deadly than the eruption. That was the case in 1953. The lahar smashed into a railway bridge, destroying it completely. Someone driving by saw what had happened. He also saw that a train was coming. He tried to flag down the train. The conductor saw the man and tried to stop the train, but it was too late.

fun FACTS

The Lord of the Rings movies were filmed in New Zealand. Some scenes were filmed on the slopes of Ruapehu.

Ruapehu and two other volcanoes are inside Tongariro National Park. People enjoy hiking and camping near this active volcano.

Hot mud bubbles in Rotorua on North Island. There are many of these bubbling hot mud pools in the parks around Rotorua.

The first part of the train nose-dived into the river. One car was left dangling. Some people escaped, but more than 150 people died in the accident.

Ruapehu continues to erupt. A ten-minute eruption in September 2007 sent ash and dust 15,000 feet into the air.

Hot Springs

Would you take a bath in smelly, muddy water? People in New Zealand do. There are hot springs on both North and South Islands. The most popular hot springs are in Rotorua (roh-toh-roo-ah) on North Island.

Rotorua is famous for its hot springs and mud pools. It is also famous for its odor. The town smells like rotten eggs! The smell bubbles up from the hot water. Many people brave the smell to soak in the natural hot springs. They think it is good for their health. Besides, it feels nice, even if it is stinky.

Geysers

Geysers are a special kind of hot spring. There are very few of them in the world. Instead of forming a pool, the hot water shoots up high into the sky. This happens

Reputedly known as the longest place name in the world

TAUMATAWHAKATANGI HANGAKOAUAUOTAMATEA TURIPUKAKAPIKIMAUNGA HORONUKUPOKAIWHEN UAKITANATAHU

THE PLACE WHERE TAMATEA, THE MAN WITH THE BIG KNEES, WHO SLID, CLIMBED, AND SWALLOWED MOUNTAINS, KNOWN AS LANDEATER, PLAYED HIS FLUTE TO HIS LOVED ONE.

"Guinness Book of Records"

A sign explains the Maori name for a hill near Porangahau, Hawke's Bay.

Hot water from geysers in New Zealand can erupt higher than 50 feet into the air.

Tourists can explore two glaciers on New Zealand's South Island: Fox Glacier and Franz Josef Glacier. A glacier is like a moving river of ice. It is not solid or flat like a sheet of paper. There are deep cracks in the ice, and shapes that look like frozen waves.

when a hot spring cannot flow freely upward but is forced through a small opening. Hot water and steam erupt, like lava from a volcano.

The word *geyser* comes from Iceland, which also has geysers. About half the world's geysers are in Yellowstone National Park in the United States.

New Zealand

More than one-quarter
of the country's people
live in the city of
Auckland, on North
Island.

New Zealand Life

By 2008, New Zealand was home to more than 4 million people, including Maori and **Pakeha** (pah-kee-hah). Pakeha are non-Maori New Zealanders. Most Pakeha have ancestors from England and other places in Europe.

Enjoying the Great Outdoors

Kiwis like to go hiking and camping. Tramping (hiking) in New Zealand is popular with both Kiwis and tourists. Many of these hikes take several days to complete. Trampers sleep in huts along the way, or they camp out in tents.

Sailing is popular, too. Auckland (AWK-land), which is New Zealand's most populated city, is known as the City of Sails.

America's Cup Trophy

New Zealand is famous for its world-class sailors and boat designers.

New Zealand Wins the America's Cup

The America's Cup is a famous **international** sailing race. It is held every five years. The first one was in England in 1851. The race sounds as though it were named for the United States of America, but that is not true. The race was named for the American sailing ship *America*. The *America* won the race that first year. American racing teams continued to win the America's Cup until 1983.

In 1995, New Zealand won the America's Cup. They won the race again in 2000. This was a tremendous achievement. Up until that time, only the United States had won the America's Cup two times in a row.

Government and Women

New Zealand is a democracy. The people elect their leaders. Women in New Zealand got the right to vote in 1893. That was twenty-seven years before American women won that same right.

The Prime Minister's offices are in this round building, called the Beehive because of the way it looks. The Beehive is in Wellington, on the southern tip of North Island. Wellington is the capital of New Zealand.

New Zealand honored Edmund Hillary by putting his picture on their five-dollar bill. He became known as "Sir Ed" after he was knighted by the queen of England in 1953.

In 2008, the leader of New Zealand's government was a woman: Prime Minister Helen Clark. She became the second woman prime minister of New Zealand when she was elected in 1999. The first woman prime minister was Jenny Shipley, who took office in 1997.

Edmund Hillary, On Top of the World

Mount Everest, on the border of Nepal and Tibet, China, is the highest place on Earth. In 1953, Edmund

Hillary and his guide from Tibet were the first people to stand on top of Mount Everest.

Hillary grew up in New Zealand. He worked as a beekeeper. For fun, he climbed mountains in New Zealand. Then he climbed mountains in other parts of the world.

Hillary became famous for climbing Everest. He had other adventures, too, including a trip to the South Pole. Hillary died in January 2008, at the age of eighty-eight.

Maori Customs and Traditions Today

Maori culture and traditions are alive today. Both English and Maori, as well as New Zealand Sign Language, are the official languages of New Zealand.

Edmund Hillary statue

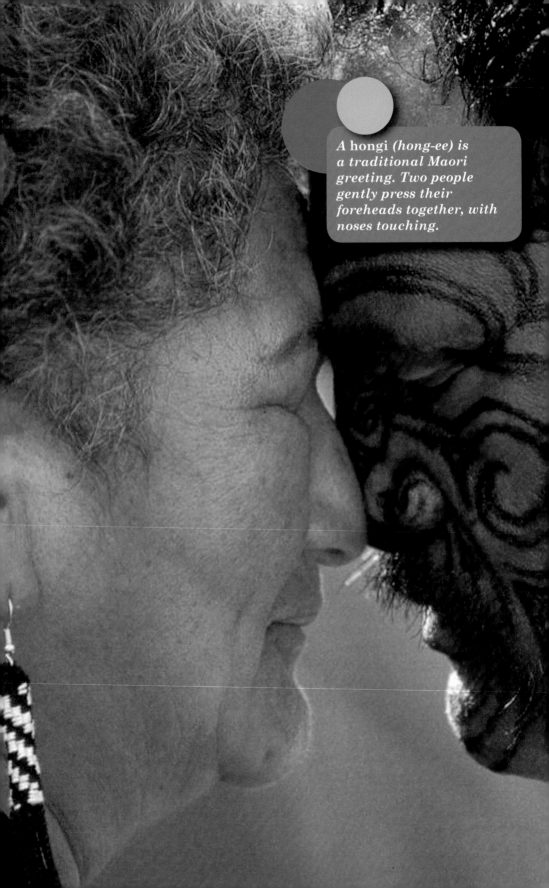

A hongi (hong-ee) is a traditional Maori greeting. Two people gently press their foreheads together, with noses touching.

The New Zealand All Blacks rugby team performs a *haka* (hah-kah) before each game. A *haka* is a war dance. It is supposed to scare the enemy—or the opposing rugby team.

A *marae* (mah-rye) is the sacred space in front of a Maori meeting house. At the heart of Maori culture, the marae is a place for weddings and other celebrations. Pakeha may enter a marae only with permission. There is a special ceremony to welcome visitors to a marae. Singing is an important part of this ceremony.

A *moko* (moh-koh) is a traditional Maori tattoo. It shows that the person is important. The first mokos were cut into the skin using a bone tool. It was painful and bloody. The cuts took a long time to heal.

Cricket is New Zealand's most popular summer sport. The game comes from England and is also played in Australia and other former British colonies around the world. It is a ball and bat game, like baseball, but the rules are very different.

"Kia Ora, Tui"

Chapter 5

Fred was early to school Monday.

"New Zealand did have dinosaurs!" Kyle told Fred as he walked into the classroom. Kyle was excited about sharing what he had found out about New Zealand dinosaurs with the rest of the class.

Fred helped Olivia hang a banner to welcome their new classmate. The banner said KIA ORA, which means "welcome" in Maori. They had decorated the banner with drawings of a silver fern. Fred had discovered that this large, lacy plant was a symbol of New Zealand. He had learned a lot about New Zealand since Mr. Lorenz had written those words on the board last week.

Fred and Olivia were admiring their work when Mr. Lorenz walked in with the

Allosaurus

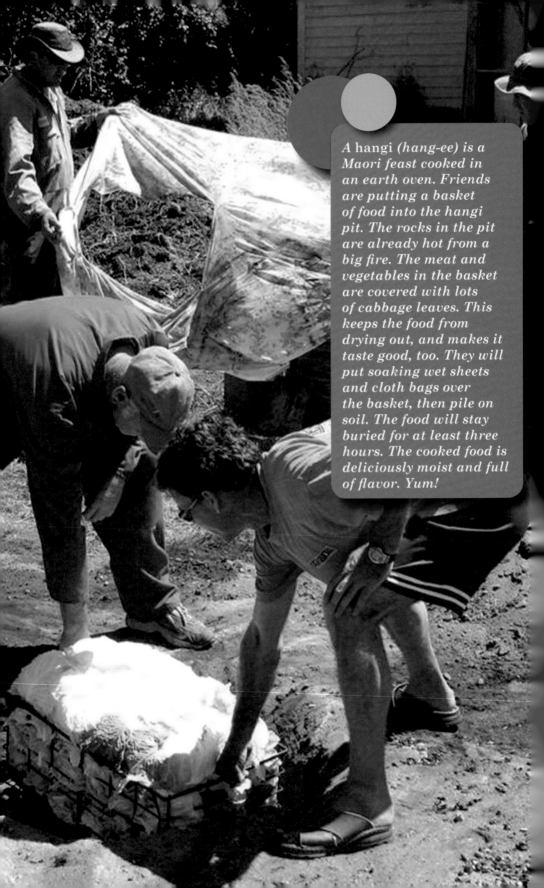

A hangi (hang-ee) is a Maori feast cooked in an earth oven. Friends are putting a basket of food into the hangi pit. The rocks in the pit are already hot from a big fire. The meat and vegetables in the basket are covered with lots of cabbage leaves. This keeps the food from drying out, and makes it taste good, too. They will put soaking wet sheets and cloth bags over the basket, then pile on soil. The food will stay buried for at least three hours. The cooked food is deliciously moist and full of flavor. Yum!

Tui plays on the beach near her house on South Island.

new student from New Zealand. He said, "Everyone, I'd like you to meet Tui."

"*Kia ora,* Tui," the class said together.

"What does your name mean?" Dylan asked.

Tui explained that her parents named her after a kind of bird that lives in New Zealand.

"That's like my name," said Robin.

"We have a surprise!" Dylan announced. He brought out a big cake.

Fred loved cake, but he had never seen one like this before. It looked a bit like a lopsided strawberry shortcake with extra kiwi fruit on top.

"A pavlova!" Tui grinned.

"What's a pavlova?" asked Robin.

"It's the national dessert of New Zealand," said Ethan.

"It's also delicious," said Dylan, licking a bit of cream off his fingers.

Fred was proud of himself and his class. They had learned a lot about New Zealand. And now that Tui was in their class, they would learn even more.

Little Penguin

How To Make
Pavlova

Instructions

Preheat oven to 225°F.

Line a large baking pan with parchment paper.

Separate the eggs, putting only the whites in a large bowl. Save the yolks for another recipe.

Beat the egg whites and cream of tartar together until soft and fluffy.

Add sugar and cornstarch slowly and continue to beat until stiff. Spoon this mixture onto the parchment paper in the shape of a circle. Make a slight, bowl-shaped dip in the center.

Ask an adult to put the pan on the center rack of the oven. Bake for 45 minutes to 1 hour. The pavlova should not darken. If it does, turn the heat down to 175°F. When the pavlova turns a pale cream color, turn off the oven. Leave the pavlova in the closed oven for 15 minutes more. It is normal for the pavlova to crack a bit. Let it finish cooling on a counter.

Spoon whipped cream onto the cooled pavlova. Decorate with kiwi fruit and berries.

Things You Will Need

Electric mixer
Parchment paper
Large baking pan
Oven
An adult to help you

Ingredients

4 eggs

¼ teaspoon cream of tartar

1 cup superfine sugar

2 teaspoons cornstarch

1 cup heavy cream, whipped with ½ teaspoon vanilla

1 cup kiwi fruit, peeled and sliced

1 cup berries, washed and dried

Make Your Own
Maori Kite for Decoration

You Will Need

Craft Sticks

String

Construction Paper or Tissue Paper

Scissors

Glue

Markers

Leaves, Twigs, Feathers, Shells (optional)

The Maori used kites to communicate with people far away. Kites are also part of the Maori New Year celebration. Maori kites were made from tree branches, bark, and other natural materials. These kites could be as big as a person, or even larger, and they were different shapes. Some looked like birds. Children's kites were smaller. People decorated their kites with shells, feathers, and colorful patterns. Not all the kites flew very well, but they were pretty to see.

Instructions for Making
A Maori Kite for Decoration

1 Make a frame for your kite using twigs or craft sticks. Use string to tie the twigs together. Your kite can be any shape or size you want.

2 Instead of using bark or wood to cover your kite, you will use paper. Use glue to paste the construction paper or tissue paper to your kite's frame.

3 Color the paper if you like. Decorate your kite with feathers , leaves, or shells. Then hang it on a door or wall so that everyone can enjoy it!

Further Reading

Books

Di Piazza, Francesca. *New Zealand In Pictures*. Visual Geography. Minneapolis: Lerner Publications, 2005.

Shepherd, Donna Walsh. *New Zealand*. Enchantment of the World. Mankato, Minnesota: Children's Press, 2002.

Te Kanawa, Kiri. *Land of the Long White Cloud: Maori Myths, Tales and Legends*. London, England: Pavilion Books, 1997.

Theunissen, Steve. *The Maori of New Zealand* (First Peoples). Minneapolis: Lerner Publications, 2002.

On the Internet

Prime Minister of New Zealand: Helen Clark
http://www.primeminister.govt.nz/index.html

RANGIKAINGA Panui, Newsletter issue 16, 2005
http://www.tangatawhenua.com/rangikainga/issue16.htm#hakinakina

Te Ara Encyclopedia of New Zealand
http://www.teara.govt.nz/en

Works Consulted

Author Ann Weil spent two years in New Zealand. This book was written from her personal experiences there. She also consulted with native New Zealanders, who are friends of hers, and the following sources for the facts in this book.

Booz, Elizabeth, and Andrew Hempstead. *New Zealand: Snowy Peaks to Ocean Deep*. New York: W.W. Norton & Co., 2006.

Chambers, John H. *A Traveller's History of New Zealand and the South Pacific Islands*. Second Edition. Northampton, Massachusetts: Interlink Books, 2007.

Further Reading

CIA. *The World Factbook: New Zealand*
    https://www.cia.gov/library/publications/
    the-world-factbook/geos/nz.html

New Zealand. London: Insight Guides, 2007.

Oettli, Peter. *Culture Shock: A Survival
    Guide to Customs and Etiquette in New
    Zealand*. Tarrytown, New York: Marshall
    Cavendish, 2006.

Consulate

New Zealand Consulate-General,
Los Angeles

2425 Olympic Blvd, Suite 600E

Santa Monica, CA 90404

Phone: 310-566-6555

Fax: 310-566-6556

Email: contact@nzcgla.com

Web Site: http://www.nzcgla.com/new/
index.php

Embassy

New Zealand Embassy

37 Observatory Circle, NW

Washington, DC 20008

Phone: 202-328-4800

Fax: 202-667-5227

Email: info@nzemb.org

Web Site: http://www.nzembassy.com/
home.cfm?c=31

Glossary

British Crown—The power of the king or queen of England.

crater (KRAY-tur)—A deep, bowl-shaped hole in the earth, often made by a volcano.

Dutch—People from the Netherlands, a country in Europe.

haka (hah-kah)—A Maori war dance.

hangi (hang-ee)—An earth oven.

hongi (hong-ee)—A traditional Maori greeting in which two people gently press their foreheads together, with noses touching.

hot springs—Naturally heated water from deep underground that bubbles to the surface.

industry (IN-dus-tree)—Business of producing useful things.

international (in-ter-NAA-shuh-nul)—Involving many countries.

kia ora (k'ee-ah or-ah)—A Maori greeting that can mean "hello," "welcome," "thank you," or "to your health!"

lahar (LAH-har)—A fast-moving mudflow from a volcano.

Maori (maw-or-ee)—Polynesian people who came to New Zealand about 500 years before Europeans arrived there.

mythical (MIH-thih-kul)—Based on myths (stories) instead of history.

Pakeha (pah-kee-hah)—Non-Maori New Zealanders.

treaty (TREE-tee)—A signed agreement between two groups who were at war or were involved in a disagreement.

Index

Ann Weil in a cave at the Franz Josef
Glacier on New Zealand's South Island.
Photo by Ann's New Zealand guide.

ABOUT THE AUTHOR

Ann Weil has written more than
50 books for children. She lived
and traveled in New Zealand for
two years and has many friends
who still live there. Now Ann hails
from New Hampshire.